BULLETPROOF MINDSET

HAVING THE RIGHT MENTAL ATTITUDE TO BE SUCCESSFUL

FIRST EDITION: APRIL 2019
PRINTED IN THE UNITED STATES OF AMERICA
ISBN-13: 9780996931441
PUBLISHED BY OMEDIO IN LOS ANGELES, CA

COPYRIGHT © 2019 BY ANGEL OLVERA, JR.
ALL RIGHTS RESERVED.

IN ACCORDANCE WITH THE U.S. COPYRIGHT ACT OF 1976, THE SCANNING, UPLOADING, AND ELECTRONIC SHARING OF ANY PART OF THIS BOOK WITHOUT THE PERMISSION OF THE PUBLISHER IS UNLAWFUL PIRACY AND THEFT OF THE AUTHOR'S INTELLECTUAL PROPERTY. IF YOU WOULD LIKE TO USE MATERIAL FROM THE BOOK (OTHER THAN FOR REVIEW PURPOSES), PRIOR WRITTEN PERMISSION MUST BE OBTAINED BY CONTACTING THE AUTHOR AT **BUSINESS@ANGELOLVERA.COM.** THANK YOU FOR YOUR SUPPORT OF THE AUTHOR'S RIGHTS.

To my circumstances that I grew up in and to all those who mentored me along the way.

TABLE OF CONTENTS

CHAPTER 1. A FEW IMPORTANT THINGS............ 7
CHAPTER 2. HOME FIELD ADVANTAGE.......... 15
CHAPTER 3. MINDSETS............ 23
CHAPTER 4. DREAMER MINDSET.......... 27
CHAPTER 5. FOLLOWER MINDSET.......... 33
CHAPTER 6. PRODUCTIVE MINDSET.......... 37
CHAPTER 7. ANGRY MINDSET.......... 43
CHAPTER 8. SHORT TERM MINDSET.......... 47
CHAPTER 9. CREATIVE MINDSET.......... 53
CHAPTER 10. GREEDY MINDSET.......... 59
CHAPTER 11. GRATITUDE MINDSET.......... 65
CHAPTER 12. CONFIDENT MINDSET.......... 71
CHAPTER 13. JEALOUS MINDSET.......... 79
CHAPTER 14. LAZY MINDSET.......... 85
CHAPTER 15. BUSINESS MINDSET.......... 91
CHAPTER 16. FEAR MINDSET.......... 95
CHAPTER 17. NETWORKING MINDSET.......... 101
CHAPTER 18. DEVELOPMENT MINDSET.......... 105
CHAPTER 19. BULLETPROOF MINDSET.......... 111
#BULLETPROOFMINDSET.......... 116
YOUR NOTE PAGES.......... 118

CHAPTER 1

A FEW IMPORTANT THINGS

Jim Carrey

Very few people knew that he was struggling with Dyslexia. His teachers used to call him disruptive and balancing school was not easy. At 10, he sent his resume to actress/comedienne Carol Burnette, hoping to be discovered. He was 14 when his father lost his job and his family was forced to live in a van. To help his family and to support his education, he took a full time factory job. At 15, he performed on stage for the first time at the Toronto comedy club in a suit made by his mother. He wasn't a hit but he didn't give up!

He used to visit Mulholland Drive every night and here is where he used to visualize his success. He wrote a $10,000,000 check to himself for "Acting Services" and used to keep the check in his pocket which was the source of motivation for him.

He eventually scored the lead role in **"The Duck Factory"** and the rest is history!

Chapter 1: A Few Important Things

THE TRUTH

I'm pretty sure you've read motivational books that promise to tell you the secret to success. Those books always claim that "once you read this book and share it with 10 people, you'll immediately start a successful new business or get that promotion you've been wanting with the office in the corner." With how many times we've heard that, I think all of us have figured out that there's no quick and easy way to achieving success. Yeah, you need to dream big and have vision, but you also need to realize that a book isn't going to make you an overnight success.

Achieving your goals only happens through planning, practice, and hard work, it's not gonna happen overnight. But all that sweat, sacrifice, and elbow grease is the reason your success is gonna be so awesome in the end!

There's a cool story about Muhammad Ali when he beat Sonny Liston for the heavyweight boxing title in 1964. Liston had knocked out the previous champ, Floyd Patterson, in the first round two years before this fight. Ali shocked the world when he beat Liston, who was the "on paper" favorite. Nobody thought he could do it. But Ali beat him in just six rounds. Suddenly, Ali became the heavyweight champion and the most famous athlete in the world. After the fight, someone asked Ali, "Not bad for a night's work, eh?"

Chapter 1: A Few Important Things

He answered that he didn't win the fight that night… not exactly. Winning the fight was a result of his hard work and preparation. "I won this fight three months ago when I decided to train to beat this man," he said.

The truth is that success is the buildup of several small wins that over time build up momentum and take on a life of their own. Success is not about one big event; it's about shifting your mindset so that you do pretty good, every single day and create a tidal wave of positivity that makes success a habit, as natural and powerful a force as momentum.

MOMENTUM

When any object has momentum, when it is in motion, it remains in motion unless it's interrupted by another force. This simple idea applies to achieving success. YOU are that other force. YOU create or interrupt the momentum of your life's journey. If you want to move forward, you'll move forward. If you want to remain in place, that's where you'll stay. The only force that can start or stop your momentum is yourself. In other words, if you keep doing what you're doing, you're gonna keep getting what you're getting.

Imagine that your life is like a blank canvas, you're your own Picasso. You need to start painting something positive and creative on that canvas every day, no matter how small it is. You're going to find that when you make all those positive strokes with your paintbrush, the canvas starts to take on a life of its own. Every little thing we do, affects whether we will accomplish our goals in life. With every positive act, you're putting pennies in the bank of success - confidence pennies, self-esteem pennies, positivity pennies. When you put those pennies in your bank everyday, over time, you're going to build yourself a fortune and success, both professionally and personally.

FINDING A MENTOR

It's so important as you're starting out to find a mentor. Now, it doesn't necessarily have to be in person. When I was learning about what I wanted and how to be a leader, I found an amazing mentor, John C. Maxwell. Now, I had never met him, but I found his books at the bookstore, started reading, and started my new education. I was becoming a leader, and I had a whole new set of things to learn so I could be the best for my people. I read his books, listened to his audios, and just took in everything he could teach me… and I never even met the guy! It was years before I got the chance meet him, and now I can say that I've worked with him on several projects in Atlanta and Florida. I even got to go with him to an Atlanta Braves game. Here I was, eating nachos and chatting with someone that I have been looking up to for years,

Chapter 1: A Few Important Things

someone that had taught me so much about mindset, leadership, and about influencing others. We had dugout seats, the best you could have, and we never actually made it to our seats because we were having so much fun hanging out! We talked and laughed and just had a great time but this was an amazing moment for me; it showed me that if you're dedicated to your dreams and you have the drive to achieve them, your mentors can in fact become your peers!

Find a mentor, master your craft, don't worry about being a perfectionist, and practice the basics. I'll give you an example: basketball. You need to learn how to dribble, how to do layups, passes, defending, etc. If you watch what all the players are doing BEFORE a basketball game starts, they're out there practicing those exact things, the fundamentals. You can acquire all the knowledge you need nowadays on your phone! Download an audiobook app and start grabbing whatever you can. I, of course, recommend John C. Maxwell but there are several other amazing mindset gurus out there that will give you the the basics for you to get started with your dreams.

CONSISTENCY

And remember, It's not about being perfect, it's about being consistent. A lot of people are too worried about being perfect and then they don't do anything. They never

Chapter 1: A Few Important Things

go anywhere. You just gotta be consistent at the process. I'll give you the example of Tom Brady. Tom Brady had a coach where he's from, San Mateo, CA, who he would visit twice a year to make sure he understood and was good at the basics and to make sure he was wired the right way, throwing the football down the hallway. He just wanted to be consistent in the fundamentals first. You gotta be bad before you're good, good before you're great, but first you gotta start. Being a perfectionist is funny. I love my wife to death, but that's her thing, she wants to be perfect before she does anything. That's the thing, it will never be perfect! You just gotta put out what you got and then adapt. It's like me doing this book, it ain't perfect but I'm going to do my best to add value to your life and in turn, grow myself. But some people are always getting ready to get ready.

GET OUT OF YOUR COMFORT ZONE

Actually doing the work is uncomfortable. But being uncomfortable is great because that means you're growing. If you're comfortable, you're complacent. If you're uncomfortable, that means you're doing something, some type of activity to grow yourself. If you have to adjust things as you go, you'll figure it out along the way.

My brother and I got the idea of starting a franchise. I had never owned one and didn't know what to do. I went online, did some research, saw the cost, talked to my

Chapter 1: A Few Important Things

brother, and we got it and figured it out along the way. We started in insurance and neither of us had ever even done insurance, but we figured it out! We just did it. We built it, learned, then sold it, it was great! We got the idea in November, and had already bought 3 locations by December, then opened on February 1. I never had any sort of background in anything like that. I had invested in other businesses but never something like that. Idea, execution, learning. Was it the business of choice? Probably not but we knew we would figure it out along the way. It was a great learning experience. I don't know why we wanted to start a traditional business. What a headache, but we learned about franchising, auto insurance, business, having a retail storefront, and through this experience, we learned so much. We did the franchise training but ultimately you're pretty much on your own. It was pretty much sink or swim. Sometimes people want to start a business because they like what they're doing. However they soon find out the business takes the fun out of what they do. I know a few personal trainers that have opened their own gyms. They love to train people and see the results but when they opened a gym, things changed. Because now, they have to wear so many hats. Business hat, accounting hat, human resources hat, AND they're trainers and it takes the fun out of it.

    Let's get started with one of the most important things BEFORE we dive into the different mindsets, the Home Field Advantage.

CHAPTER REVIEW

- Success isn't going to happen overnight. It takes planning, practice, and hard work.
- Success is the buildup of several small wins over time.
- Success is about shifting your mindset.
- YOU create the momentum of your life's journey. If you remain in place, that's where you'll stay.
- It's so important to find yourself a mentor.
- Practice the basics.
- Remember, it's not about being perfect, it's about being consistent.
- If you're uncomfortable, you're doing something to help you grow.

CHAPTER 2

HOME FIELD ADVANTAGE

Michael Jordan

At the age of 15, while a sophomore in high school, Jordan was passed up for the varsity basketball team, instead being assigned to the junior varsity team. He cried after he saw that list without his name on it. But instead of giving up, his mom convinced him to push forward. Every time he thought about stopping his training, he would picture that list without his name on it.

He was able to take failure in stride. He allowed it to push him rather than to entirely defeat him. At the age of 21, he entered the NBA as a professional basketball player for the Chicago Bulls, where he would go on to win six championship titles and become one of the most impactful players to ever play the game.

Chapter 2: Home Field Advantage

Home field advantage is having the right environment to become successful. It's not just going out there and having an idea and trying to make it happen. You have to have a support system. Think about a young kid somewhere out there in the world who could have been the next Michael Jordan, the next Mia Hamm, the next sitcom star, or the next Grammy winning artist. However, while the kid was singing around the house into the remote control, their parents who are supposed to be their support system, told the kid to shut up. Maybe the parent was having a bad day and said "Hey, you're really annoying, be quiet!" Imagine what those words could do to that kid's mindset? Right there could have been the next Grammy winner for best song of the year, but instead they got a sense of fear and doubt for what they loved to do. Or think about a kid that was outside, bouncing a baseball off the wall of the house. The parents would come out and say, "What are you doing?! Stop doing that, that's annoying!" Imagine having that drip into your mindset at such a young age. It can create fear, hostility, doubt, anger, shame, shyness, a whole bunch of different negative feelings because it's coming from the people that are your support system as you're growing up, your home field. That can have some serious effects long term. I know people that to this day are still affected by thoughts like that coming from their support system when they were kids.

I remember when I was starting out in business, trying to become successful, I didn't have a positive support

Chapter 2: Home Field Advantage

system at home. I was out trying to make things work, trying to provide a better life for my family and I would come home to someone bringing me down saying things like "It's not gonna work, you're just wasting your time. It's not gonna work." All these negative things made me question what I was doing… but my bulletproof mindset didn't bring me down. When I realized that I had so much negativity pushing down my dreams, I realized that maybe this situation, was not going to change. Maybe I had to change my Home Field. I just got to a point in my life that I realized that I was going in one direction and my Home Field was going in the complete opposite, and that is exactly what ended up happening.

Now, I've been able to become successful because of my support system, MY Home Field Advantage. My family, my wife, my kids, my friends, they understand me and understand what I do, and they support me in doing those things… they're my #1 cheerleaders! I know in the back of my mind that if I go out there into the world and give it my all to provide an amazing quality of life for my family that I can come home and have the support and love of my favorite people. That's Home Field Advantage.

Right now there's a bunch of athletes in the minor leagues, people starting new businesses, people working towards promotions, that are giving it their all, sometimes for years. The moment that they get to the next level that they desire, their lives could completely change for their families. The only way those people can soldier on and

Chapter 2: Home Field Advantage

fight for their dreams, is if they have a support system at home that is helping them push forward. If they don't, they probably will never make it to the next level.

The key to having Home Field Advantage is to make your support system a part of your process. This is why I always suggest to make a dream board together with your family. WHY do you want to be successful? WHY do you want to make it big? Maybe you want that bigger house, the bigger backyard, the better car, live in a better neighborhood. Make the dream board together. Get your family involved. Take a drive to the neighborhood that you want to live together. Take pictures in the car that you want. Don't forget that your support system is involved as much in what you're doing to become successful as you are. Maybe they're not doing the grinding part of the process but they're there when you wake up, they're there motivating you throughout the day, and they're there when your head hits the pillow.

You may be thinking about it right now and you're saying "I don't have Home Field Advantage right now. I don't have the support system I need to be successful." I've been there, and I didn't know that I was there until I was OUT of there. This is where your mindset is key. Lucky for me, I have a powerful mindset that got me through not having Home Field Advantage. Directly or indirectly, not having that support system definitely affects you, I don't care who you are. If you're trying to make it in sports, you might hear something in the back of your mind telling you

Chapter 2: Home Field Advantage

you're about to miss this goal. Or if you're doing real estate, as you're driving to the listing to setup your street signs, you hear a voice telling you again that "You're not going to sell this house." If you don't have the strong will to get you through this, you're not going to make it, you're not going to be successful.

I grew up with friends who to this day, never grew up. They think it's still 1994. They live in the past, they talk about the past and that's what their whole life is made of. They are 100% my friends and I love them but I don't let them affect my daily life. I'm not going to push them out of my life, but I'm also not going to take advice from them. I'll see them from time to time, once in a blue moon and that's fine with us. I understood I needed to surround myself with people that were going to make me raise my game. I needed to surround myself with people that were in a different league so I had the motivation to get to that next level. I didn't wanna stay in the minor leagues, I wanted to get to the majors so I needed to start playing with major league players.

Home Field Advantage is also a direct reflection of the people you hang out with the most. They say that you are who you hang out with, the law of association. I'll give you an example. When I golf with people who are really good golfers, I actually do really well. I FEEL like I'm not doing that well because those people are really good golfers but I am doing way better than I would if I was golfing with people who aren't so good. Sometimes, I'm the best golfer

Chapter 2: Home Field Advantage

out there on the green! But that's because I'm playing with people who are horrible! And that's the thing, sometimes, you may be at the TOP of your game but take a look back and make sure that you're playing the right game.

If you are the best out of your circle of friends in terms of success, it may benefit you to hang out with a different circle. That way, you aren't the most successful person, and have something to aspire to. That's what I mean about maybe having to change your Home Field. It's not because you don't wanna be friends with people anymore, it's because you aspire for more and you need that challenge from people more successful than you. I talked about being uncomfortable in the last chapter, and this situation is probably one of the MOST uncomfortable things you could do. But you don't have to do it permanently, you can do it temporarily. It's ok to do that.

The bottom line is support. Whether you're a real estate mogul that's traveling all over the country to sell commercial land or you're the company CFO pulling late nights and early mornings or you're an athlete with games all over the world, if you don't have Home Field Advantage, if you don't have that support system, it's going to affect you.

Maybe YOU'RE the person that needs to be supporting someone. In that case, know that they're doing this not only for themselves but also for you. Let them know that they can do whatever they put their mind to, that they have the desire and work ethic to do it but they also have the

Chapter 2: Home Field Advantage

support system in you while they're out there building their dreams.

    I know people personally that could fly if they had the right Home Field Advantage. Some I'm related to, some are friends. Knowing what I know now about Home Field Advantage, it's kind of sad knowing that they could be so amazing if they just had the support they needed.

    Now, you can have the absolute best Home Field Advantage in the world… but if you're lazy, it's useless. Even if you have amazing support and love at home, if you don't get up, step up, and play the game, you ain't going anywhere.

CHAPTER REVIEW

- Home Field Advantage is having the right environment to become successful.
- A negative support system can affect your entire life.
- Don't let people stuck in their past bring you back with them.
- The key to having Home Field Advantage is to make your support system a part of the process.
- Home Field Advantage is also a direct reflection of the people you hang out with the most, the law of association.
- Sometimes, you may have to reflect on your Home Field and adjust accordingly, even if it's temporary.

CHAPTER 3

MINDSETS

Sara Blakely

Blakely graduated from Florida State University with a Bachelor's degree in communications. She had various jobs while working at Disney World before she became the first salesperson and then national sales trainer for Danka, an office-supply company.

While in search of a comfortable undergarment that would make her appear slimmer and was undetectable beneath her clothing, she cut off the feet of a pair of panty hose and found that she created something that other women would want. She used her $5,000 personal savings to market her new invention and worked days at Danka but spent her nights researching fabrics, patents, designs, and other important aspects of her new invention. Eventually, she found a company that would produce her invention, wrote her own patent application, and her branding.

Then, in late 2000, Oprah Winfrey featured Blakely's new invention, Spanx, on her TV show and her sales began to skyrocket. Shortly after, Sara Blakely built an empire, all without advertising or outside investment. Her sales experience allowed her to be her own model on TV and in public store appearances for Spanx. By early 2012, her company, which was solely owned by her, reached a value of $1 Billion.

Chapter 3: Mindsets

The following chapters in this book will allow you to recognize the different kinds of mindsets. This is not a definitive list but a list that I've compiled over the years from my own personal growth as well as what I've experienced working with people. These are the important ones. You'll be able to identify which mindsets you've been in, which ones you're in now, and maybe where you want to go. You'll also learn how to adjust those mindsets to benefit your current situation. I believe that if you're not AWARE of negative things, you won't be able to get out of those things.

You'll even learn how so many different things can affect your mindset. From simple things like your coffee place getting your favorite drink wrong to more complicated things like allowing your upbringing to dictate your future.

As you go through these mindsets, I'll admit, you're probably going to feel uncomfortable. That's because you're going to realize some things about yourself that you hadn't before. You're going to have 'aha' moments where you realize the type of mindset that's holding you back from getting that promotion, from getting onto the team, from achieving that next level in business… but you're also going to realize the type of mindset that you need to be successful.

Some people have something called a fixed mindset. A person with a fixed mindset is basically someone who already thinks they know everything and doesn't see the benefit in growing. This was definitely me before I started

Chapter 3: Mindsets

to have my own personal growth journey. I was who I was and that was it! That's true even with the little things. I would buy something that you were supposed to build at home and the first thing I would do after opening the box was throw the instructions away.

As I began to write this book, I was reflecting on myself and all the different mindsets I've been in and out of. I used to be the kid that would go up to bat and think to myself, "I'm gonna hit it out of the park." And now, when I'm about to go on stage in front of thousands of people, I tell myself "I'm gonna kill it on stage." I didn't know as a kid what I was doing but I was psyching myself up to whatever task I was about to do. And when I'm backstage now, I see people doing jumping jacks, pushups, with headphones on playing their favorite song, or just talking to themselves, all psyching themselves up the same way I was.

I've been in my personal growth journey for about 20 years. I've had downs and ups all throughout my life and I've tried to learn something from each experience. They say that if you're not growing, you're dying. This book is going to teach you how to have a bulletproof mindset, even when people on the freeway cut you off, or your spouse tells you that your new business venture isn't going to work, or your friend on social media went on that vacation that you had planned for yourself.

I wrote this book to save you the trouble of figuring things out the hard way. Let's start learning about the different kinds of mindsets.

Chapter 3: Mindsets

CHAPTER REVIEW

- There are many types of mindsets that you can be in.
- The key is to identify which mindset you're in and adjust depending on the situation.
- Don't let things affect your mindset. Don't let a small detail ruin your whole day.
- Fixed mindset vs growth mindset
- If you're about to do something that brings you fear, psych yourself up. You can use music, talk to yourself, or simply do some jumping jacks or pushups.
- The key is to have a Bulletproof Mindset.

CHAPTER 4

DREAMER MINDSET

Mary Kay Ash

After marrying early on in life, in 1935, at the age of 17, she became a housewife, had two children, and would sell books door-to-door when her husband was fighting in the war.

In 1945, she divorced and went to work for a company called Stanley Home Products. She retired at the age of 45-years old and decided to write a book. That book turned into what would be her business plan for the business she intended to start with her new husband, Mel Ash, however he died just a month before the new business was set to start. She took the plunge by taking a $5,000 investment from her eldest son and opened up her first storefront in Dallas and created the company to help empower women to succeed in a marketplace that was dominated by men.

Mary Kay Cosmetics grew beyond her wildest dreams. Today, the company has over 3 million consultants around the world with sales topping $3 billion annually.

Chapter 4: Dreamer Mindset

The Dreamer mindset starts when you're little. If you look at pictures of little me, you probably won't find a picture WITHOUT a baseball in hand, a baseball glove, and a LA Dodgers shirt on. 2, 3, 4, years old, I knew that was my dream, to be a baseball player. And as you grow, your dreams change a little bit. I remember growing up in California, we used to drive down the 405 freeway, down to Santa Monica beach during summer break and I would see these huge mansions off of the freeway. We would drive through Bel Air and Brentwood, and all those places were amazing. As a young guy, I would be in total Dreamer mode. I would think, "Look at these people, what do they do? It's amazing!" And as I continued to grow, I dreamt of being able to live wherever I wanted, being able to drive the cars you see in LA that all the celebrities drove. I had that Dreamer mindset, I didn't want to have any limits. I know a lot of people that dream but then the little voice in their head or a voice around them talks them down out of their dream. Sometimes, it could even be the circumstances that you grew up in.

I remember seeing those gated communities and thinking I was going to live in one… but a slightly different gated community. The gates at the communities that I grew up in were there to stop us from going into the allies to see the drunks, the drug dealers, and the crime going on around us. It was crazy, everyone was afraid to go out at night, so bad that my family eventually got bars on our windows. Yes, in LA, we have bars on our windows. To me

Chapter 4: Dreamer Mindset

that was normal. I remember bringing a friend to LA to see where I grew up and they were shocked about that. I looked at it and said "Man, that was a luxury to have those bars! I remember the day we got those bars, it was awesome!" I guess most people would see that as a prison but it kept the bad people OUT for us.

People around me used to tell me things like "What are you talking about?" and "That's crazy, you can't travel the world." They thought I was crazy. But I didn't let it affect me. Those kinds of thoughts don't affect the Dreamer.

I always suggest that people make a Dream Board to have at home or put it out there on social media. Envision yourself in your dream. Have pictures that you've taken that allow you to SEE yourself in the future, in those dreams. Like I said in the previous chapter, put it out there. Take a picture of yourself in your dream car, go with your kid to the school that they want to go to and take a picture there. My kid had a dream to go to Stanford University. As a father who is a Dreamer, I told him "Dream big. You can go there, you can do it." And he did it! I have a little one (at the time of writing this) that wants to be an actress and we fully support her.

Here's the thing: when you are in the Dreamer mindset, you are more open minded, because the next opportunity that opens up could open the door for you to achieve your dream. If you're stuck at a job you don't like, your dream job could be right around the corner with a new opening that you just have to go look for. Or if you finally want to

Chapter 4: Dreamer Mindset

open up that restaurant that you've always wanted and the opportunity for some money is just a phone call away from someone who is looking to invest, that could be your funding for the restaurant. Or if you have a Dream spouse that you've imagined in your head, your friend's new friend that moved into town could be the person that you've been waiting for your whole life! You just have to ask them out!

    The best example I can give you is this: I didn't become a baseball player, but that didn't stop me from my dream of living like one. I got kicked out of high school and had to start work to support my kid that I had at 16 so I got a construction job. And after years of working there, I knew that working there wouldn't give me access to my dreams so I always kept my options open. I kept on the lookout for the vehicle that would open the door to have what I dreamt of. I didn't know what it was going to be but I knew it was SOMETHING. And at the age of 23, I got the opportunity I was looking for. I was introduced to a business and BOOM, I had my vehicle to my dreams. The door had opened. And I know that the only reason that business allowed me to get to my dreams was because I was waiting for it, I was searching for it. I know I needed whatever the opportunity was so that I could take it and run with it. And the rest is history.

    And whenever I would reach a dream, I would have new dreams. The Dreamer is always dreaming bigger. When I bought my first Ferrari or when I moved into my first gated community, I knew that I could have more once I got there.

Chapter 4: Dreamer Mindset

"I can dream bigger now." When I got my first status on an airline, and then I got status on multiple airlines, then I could see myself owning a jet.

The point is to have the dream in the first place. And if you aren't in the Dreamer mindset, maybe ask your kids, your spouse, your parents, whatever your Home Field is what THEY dream about. You'll quickly find a reason to be successful when it means doing it with the people you love. I remember a few years ago when I was close to hitting a milestone in my business, my father, who always supported me, had a dream to own an RV. With the success I was able to have, I was able to go and purchase him his own RV! It fueled me, it motivated me to know that someone I loved and who supported me, wanted something that I was able to then provide for him.

Chapter 4: Dreamer Mindset

CHAPTER REVIEW

- The Dreamer mindset starts when you are young.
- Dreamers are often looked at as if they're crazy and that's ok.
- Envision yourself in your dreams: make a dream board or post it on social media.
- When you're in the Dreamer mindset, you're open-minded and when an opportunity comes, you're ready.
- When you reach one of your dreams, then you can create bigger dreams. The Dreamer is always dreaming bigger.

CHAPTER 5

FOLLOWER MINDSET

Mark Cuban

In his earliest years, Cuban was always a tinkerer with an entrepreneurial spirit. From selling garbage bags to running newspapers and everything in between, Cuban learned early on how the mechanics of business worked, but that didn't mean he didn't experience the gut-wrenching pain of failure along the way. He tried numerous jobs but simply couldn't get anything right. At the age of 25, one year after he arrived in Dallas, he decided to start his own company, MicroSolutions, selling software, doing training and configuring networks and computers. He grew that company to $30 million dollars in revenue, and it was later acquired by CompuServe in 1990.

That gave him the ability to create Broadcast.com, a company that was later acquired by Yahoo for $5.7 billion in stock. Cuban was 41-years old, famous and wealthy beyond measure. Although he had failed numerous times and been through the wringer, he never gave up.

Chapter 5: Follower Mindset

There's less risk to be a follower. Most of the time, when you're in the follower mindset, you're following someone else's dream. Let me explain with an example: You go to school because "they told me to." A lot of people might not want to go to school but they do because their parents told them to. You're kinda just following. Another example is religion. Most people will be in the religion that their parents are in because that's what you do. They didn't make their own decision. Basically, you're going after what others want, not necessarily what you want. And that's what the Follower mindset is.

Don't get me wrong, you can be super happy in this mindset. You don't have much confrontation with having to make your own choices, you don't question things, it's super safe. But just know that you're following someone else's agenda. You're just going through life doing what life is "supposed" to be.

I'm sure we can all define what life is "supposed" to be: go to school, get a job, then start a family. Kind of like me, my parents wanted me to do exactly that. But I ended up getting kicked out of school, having a kid at 16, and getting a construction job because that's all I could get. Eventually, I had to go back to trade school for the construction job, because they would give me raises for every semester I completed. But still, I only went to school because that's what the construction job told me to do. And even at that construction job, my dad had expectations for me to start

Chapter 5: Follower Mindset

my own construction company or move up in the ladder with him in the union.

    Here's the thing, I was doing pretty damn good. I had a high-paying construction job, bought a house, bought cars, and had nice things. I'm not saying that being in the Follower mindset that you can't live a good life, the Follower mindset just worked for me at that time because I needed some sort of structure while the Dreamer in me waited for the right opportunity. Imagine having all that at age 20? Not so bad right? But the entire time, I was following someone else's agenda, their structure on how I was supposed to live my life. I took a step back and looked at where my life was going once I figured that out.

    And the Follower won't do that, they're content following, playing in the safe part of the pool. If a Follower does have dreams, they most likely will not act upon them. A Follower mindset doesn't really have full control over their life, but they're allowed to believe they do. It's the norm, and if you're ok with that, that's fine.

CHAPTER REVIEW

- There's less risk to be a follower.
- You can be super happy with the Follower mindset, just know that it many not necessarily be what you want.
- Reflect on yourself and see if you've been living a Follower mindset, living someone else's agenda.

CHAPTER 6

PRODUCER MINDSET

J.K. Rowling

Quite possibly one of the most famous and renowned former-failures of our time, J.K. Rowling is the author of the wildly-popular Harry Potter series of books. Born in 1965, she grew up with a tumultuous childhood that included a difficult and oftentimes-strained relationship with her father, and dealing with the illness of her mother.

It wasn't until 1996, when a small literary house in London named Bloomsbury gave her the green light. They gave her a very small advance of £1500. In 1997, seven years after the initial idea for the young wizard, the first Harry Potter book was published. By 2004, Rowling had become the first author to become a billionaire through book writing, according to Forbes.

Chapter 6: Producer Mindset

The Producer mindset is key because it allows you to get tasks done efficiently and quickly. People who are in this mindset are able to complete their goals at a much faster rate and usually don't get distracted. You are able to prioritize important tasks. In this mindset, you take the things that you don't want to do and you do them first to get them out of the way. It's like people who work out early in the morning, they get it out of the way. If you want to work out, but don't prioritize it, you'll start thinking about it and give yourself a reason not do it. And then, guess what, you don't do it! Maybe you have to make an important call and you start doing other things. No, do that call first! Get it out of the way.

Sometimes, I fall back in the trap of NOT Producing. I would leave an important task for last because I didn't want to do it and then I would either not get it done, or I'd get done sloppy. But if you want to be successful, be in the Producer mindset.

Now, people who are in the Producer mindset COULD over work themselves and that's not a good thing. You have to keep a balance when you're in the Producer mindset because if you overwork yourself, you can really hurt yourself.

For me, I learned at a young age that you can't die from hard work and whatever you lack in talent, you can make up with hard work as well. It depends on what you're trying to accomplish. Do you want to be in the top 1% at the company you work at? Do you want to break those charts

Chapter 6: Producer Mindset

in whatever sport you play? If that sounds like something you want, you HAVE to get into the Producer mindset. A good example is Kobe Bryant.

Kobe talks about the Mamba Mentality. The killer instinct. Making it happen when you don't feel like making it happen. Making that phone call when you don't want to do it. Driving to that meeting two hours away even if you don't want to.

There are Producers and non-Producers. Do what is productive that will help you get closer to achieving the goal that you're trying to get at. If you're a network marketer, get those extra customers to qualify for that next rank. If you're trying to get more leads for your company, make some calls or ads. If you want to become a better basketball player, do more layups and free throws. Do more than the average person and you'll be in that Producer mindset.

Cristiano Ronaldo, amazing soccer player, always shows up to practice before his team mates and then stays after training. Tiger Woods would golf a 4-day tournament and then would be at the range the next day working on his game. The little things that you do behind the scenes are what pays off. That's what puts you into the Producer Mindset. These people are elite and #1 producers because they do more than everyone else is willing to do.

I remember when I first started out in business, the first few years, I was in the Producer mindset 24/7. And as I got older, I toned it down a little bit but I always have it on my

Chapter 6: Producer Mindset

mind. I don't think Producer mindset people ever shut it off. If I'm watching a movie, something could spark an idea for how to do something better or a whole new idea and I'll start thinking about it.

If you're at a job, know that most people do just enough to not get fired. That's the path of least resistance. But someone in the same job with a Producer mindset might do things much quicker because they want to get it done and are able to prioritize.

From playing tee-ball at 5 years old to when I was playing in high school, I was always an All-Star. And there were people who COULD have been All-Stars but they were unwilling to work as hard as I was. I'd play a game then go home and want to play catch or bounce the ball on the wall. Just constantly doing it to get better and I didn't realize it at the time but that's what helped me become an All-Star, I was in the Producer mindset to get things done, to have the results, to be successful.

When the cameras aren't rolling, after the game is over, after all the people have left for the day, the Producers are there getting things done.

CHAPTER REVIEW

- The Producer mindset allows you to get tasks done efficiently and quickly.
- Prioritizing is key for this mindset.
- Put the most important tasks FIRST and get them out of the way.
- DON'T overwork yourself in this mindset.
- Take the examples from successful athletes who do the extra work.
- You may have to be in this mindset A LOT in the beginning but once you hit some comfortable success, you can tone back a little.

Chapter 6: Producer Mindset

CHAPTER 7

ANGRY MINDSET

Oprah Winfrey

Oprah Winfrey was born in 1954 to a single teenaged mother. Winfrey grew up in utter poverty for most of her childhood, living with her grandmother. During those early years, Winfrey says she was sexually molested by her cousin, her uncle and a family friend. At the age of 13, she ran away from home. At 14-years old, she was pregnant and gave birth prematurely to a baby that died shortly after birth.

At the age of 17, she won a beauty pageant and interned at a radio station, creating a love for the media, and eventually landing a job after college as a news anchor in Nashville. After college, she moved to Baltimore to co-anchor the news, but was later removed by the producer for being unfit for television.

Oprah was able to overcome multiple failures in her life, but didn't give up. Because of it, she reached international fame and is known around the world as a household name.

Chapter 7: Angry Mindset

I think that people who are in this mindset have had something happen to them and the only outlet that they feel they have is to pour it onto everyone else. Many times, people in this mindset are unable to control their emotions. I see this all the time.

Imagine having a car salesperson come up to you and start telling you all the bad stuff about the car you were looking at and they get so crazy that they push you away and you leave. It was probably not something against you but something that happened to them to make them treat you this way. I've grown up with people that are in this mindset. They blame everything on the circumstances that they grew up in and never get over that hump. That's just who they are. I wish they knew they could snap out of it if they developed their mindset, through personal growth. The Law of Association comes to play here as well as Home Field because if you are surrounded by angry people, they will also make you angry. And then you'll project your anger to the rest of the world and that will 100% keep you from being successful.

People in the anger mindset blame others for their failures and lack of success, but that's just not how it works. You are where you are, because of the person in the mirror.

I learned that when someone tells you that it can't be done, it's more a reflection of their limitations than yours'. I grew up on the "wrong side of the tracks." Gangs, drugs, alcohol, crime, drive by shootings, everything you can think of, but I didn't sit there and blame all that for my current

Chapter 7: Angry Mindset

situation. Some people fall victims to their circumstances and I just didn't allow it. I didn't allow my kids to fall for that either.

Now, there's an important distinction you need to understand: having angry moments and getting angry are very different than being in an angry mindset. I've never considered myself an angry person but I for sure can get angry. You can have a blowout with a coworker but then have to do a presentation and put that to the side for the sake of your success. People in an Angry mindset would not be able to do that and it would affect their success.

When I first started my business and I was trying to become successful, I would let this affect me. People would make fun of me and say negative things and I would get angry and become combative with those people. I didn't just react angrily, I began fighting those people. As I developed myself as a leader, as a business person, I learned that it wasn't me people were angry at, they were in an Angry mindset themselves and were just projecting it onto me. Once I understood that, I stopped taking it personally. For me, the more I grew, the better I was able to filter and handle things.

Simple mindset with a simple solution: look at when you're pointing a finger and realize that there's three fingers pointing right back at you.

Chapter 7: Angry Mindset

CHAPTER REVIEW

- People in this mindset pour it onto everyone else.
- Angry mindset people also blame others for their failures.
- You are where you are because of the person in the mirror, not other people.
- Remember, having angry moments and having and Angry mindset are two different things, it's ok to be angry sometimes.
- The more you grow, the better you'll be able to filter situations.
- Don't point fingers. Instead, realize that there's three fingers pointing back at you.

CHAPTER 8

SHORT TERM MINDSET

Harrison Ford

Born in 1942 in Chicago, both of Ford's parents had a connection to the entertainment industry. His father was a former actor and his mother a former radio actress. After graduating from college in Wisconsin, at the age of 22, Ford headed to Los Angeles to try his hand in voice-overs. He failed to secure that job but ended up staying in the area.

It took Ford two years of working odd jobs and small-time bits before he landed his first uncredited role as a bellhop in the movie, Dead Heat on a Merry-Go Round, in 1964 at the age of 24. However, studio execs were rough on young Ford, telling him that "he would never make it in this business."

But Ford refused to give up. It took him until 1973, 9 years later, when he landed his breakthrough role in George Lucas's film, American Graffiti. It was that role, and his relationship with Lucas, that would help catapult him into stardom. Lucas later cast Ford in Star Wars and the Indiana Jones series.

Chapter 8: Short Term Mindset

Someone who is in this mindset is addicted to things that will make them happy for a short period of time but continuing this mindset would make them miserable later in life. Sure, you'll be happy for a hot minute, but then what? John C. Maxwell said that "Everything worthwhile is uphill" and that's especially true of short term happiness.

Short term mindset equals instant gratification. That is where our society is at. Compare that to someone who is in the Dreamer mindset, that's someone who is looking at things from afar and realizing that it's going to take some time to get there and they'll have to delay that gratification. It's like when people want to lose weight with a diet. Have you ever tried one of those liquid diets, the Hollywood Diet? I've tried the lemonade and cayenne pepper diet... yeah you'll lose weight but then it comes back double the amount of what you originally lost! But for that week that you lost 10-15 pounds, you felt like you accomplished something. Yay, pat on the back, woohoo. But what happens after? When you're in the Short Term mindset, you don't think about what happens in the long run, you're just worried about right now.

It's the same in business, people want to have success but they want the success to come immediately. Some people think that by having their idea, then starting a company and having their EIN, they're ready to cash the checks. They're ready to drive a Bentley. Umm, no. It don't work like that. You gotta go and pay your dues up front and eventually it'll happen. People in the Short Term

Chapter 8: Short Term Mindset

mindset aren't patient with the process. This is very dangerous in all aspects of life: relationships, business, personal goals, everything.

Here's the thing, everyone should have short term goals, mid term goals, and long term goals. The short term goals are what gives you the little pushes to move forward because, well, you ARE moving forward. But it's when you're moving and have no idea what you're heading towards that you have a problem. And that all comes down to patience.

People with a Short Term mindset just don't have the patience. They just want to fulfill the moment. I like to compare it to people who constantly have a new boyfriend or girlfriend. I'm sure we all know someone who just seems to always be jumping from relationship to relationship. The reason they do that is that they don't have patience. They love that honeymoon stage of the beginning of a relationship but once there's some time invested and the real work of staying together starts, they part ways and move on to the next. And they wonder why they're not in a long term relationship, it's because they just like the short term results.

I can tell you that I've been in this mindset. For me, I've gotten there with my fitness. I remember specifically when I got married, I needed to lose some weight quick. I did fasting, eating almost nothing, and drinking some nasty spicy lemonade, all so I could have the weight loss super quick… but then in a month, it came back DOUBLE. It was horrible. Now, I have a regular workout routine and diet that I can manage and still be happy, and the results I have are so significant, even though I'm not following my fitness plan 100%.

It's like a Band-Aid on an open wound, a quick fix. That's actually why a lot of people get in trouble, especially in business. They want that quick buck, the get-rich-quick scheme, and they'll sometimes do illegal stuff just to get it done, but that always ends up biting you in the you-know-what in the long run.

Chapter 8: Short Term Mindset

CHAPTER REVIEW

- People in this mindset are addicted to things that will only make them happy for a short period of time.
- Everything worthwhile is uphill - John C. Maxwell
- Short term mindset people want instant gratification. They'll refuse to see in the long term.
- You're not going to have instant success. Success takes time.
- Short term goals are ok if you also have mid and long term goals.
- It comes down to patience or lack of patience.

Chapter 8: Short Term Mindset

CHAPTER 9

CREATIVE MINDSET

Sylvester Stallone

Stallone moved to New York City in the 1970's to pursue his dream of being an actor. However, all he seemed to face was rejection, failure and a string of people telling him he talked funny, walked funny, and couldn't act.

He was broke at the time. It was during this period that he was forced to sell his dog for $25 just to pay for his electricity bill. He had been rejected 1,500 times by talent scouts, agents and everyone in the film industry that he could get a meeting with. He would sit for hours in offices just to wait to the see the person who would ultimately reject him again. He did this repeatedly. He was broke and homeless. He was just about as desperate as anyone could be in their lives.

After writing the script for Rocky, he was offered a tremendous amount of money with one caveat — that he not star in the film. The offer was raised as high as $325,000 with the condition that he not act in the film. He refused time and again. Eventually, he accepted $35,000 and a percentage of the film's sales which grossed over $200 million in the box office!

Chapter 9: Creative Mindset

Being creative is more difficult than it seems. The reason for that is when I say creative, I mean someone who can think outside the box. But sometimes, the Creative mindset is SO creative that it's difficult for them to do their best work. They over think and try to reinvent the wheel.

A lot of times, people think they're being creative when they're really just replicating ideas they've seen before. For example, in business the best thing you can do in business is replicate a successful system. In my main business, we have a system for success. If you follow the system to a tee, you should experience success. The problem with the Creative mindset is that you try to do your own thing that goes away from the system and suddenly, you don't have the results you want.

But here's the thing, people in the Creative mindset are excellent problem solvers. Problems will always arise in whatever part of your life that you're trying to be successful at. Thats when you want to turn on the Creative mindset and solve the problems in a way that benefits everyone. With this mindset, you'll think outside the box to solve the problem at hand. I've told people before, if you have a better way of doing things, go do it and THEN we can change the system. But until that happens, you have to follow the system. Everyone is open to new ideas but you have to SHOW the way first before you start changing things.

I'll give you an example: McDonalds. McDonalds has a system. When you go to to a McDonalds, the fry machine

Chapter 9: Creative Mindset

is on the left, coke machine on the right. Every McDonalds you go to has that. They aren't in the burger business, they're in the distribution business and the system they established is what lets them be so successful.

Whataburger has a system, White Castle has a system, Shake Shack has a system, and the best burger place ever, In-n-Out, has a system (sorry, I'm from California and they're the best).

For me, I've never been too creative. I've always understood blueprints and ways to do things based on systems and I've thrived at that. When I play golf, sure I have my own style but there are golf coaches that will analyze your swing and tell you what to tweak to have the perfect swing. The perfect swing gives you the maximum results when you're playing. I don't see how someone can reinvent the golf swing to make it better, you just get better at trying to achieve the perfect swing, the system for golf. Athletes practice the basics because it's the system.

It's like Phil Jackson. Phil Jackson is a basketball coach who created the triangle system that he used with the Chicago Bulls. He won SIX titles with the Bulls using that system. And then he came over to the Los Angeles Lakers and brought the same system and won FIVE more titles. He got his players to follow the system and they were insanely successful. I'm sure there were some players that were so good that they probably had a better way of doing things but they had to follow the system to be successful.

Chapter 9: Creative Mindset

As a leader though, I'm a problem solver. I jump into the Creative mindset when it comes to creating systems that work. I would have made a great engineer because I love to solve problems and develop systems that work and will continue to work. In my business organization, I helped create the system we use and when people follow it, they're crazy successful. I've had people that have never done the kind of business that I do make millions of dollars because they followed the system.

The Creative mindset is a powerful mindset to be able to turn on and off depending on the situation. Just remember to not forget about doing the simple things the right way.

Chapter 9: Creative Mindset

CHAPTER REVIEW

- People in the Creative mindset are excellent problem solvers because they think outside the box to find a solution.
- But they have a tendency to over think and try to reinvent the wheel when it comes to simple stuff.
- If there is a system in place for you to be successful, follow the system while using the Creative mindset to solve problems along the way.
- The Creative mindset is best when you're able to turn it on and off, depending on the situation.
- Don't forget to keep the simple things simple.

Chapter 9: Creative Mindset

CHAPTER 10

GREEDY MINDSET

Barbara Corcoran

Barbara Corcoran grew up as the 2nd oldest of 10 kids in a poor area of New Jersey. Her credentials include straight D's in school and twenty jobs by the time she turned 23.

While working as a waitress in New Jersey, her boyfriend loaned her $1,000 to start a business showing rentals to people in Manhattan, NY. Eventually, she realized that sales had higher commissions and immediately started selling.

In 1978, her then husband who loaned her the first $1,000 said he was leaving her and that she would "Never succeed" without him. This made her work harder than ever before and after struggling with cash flow for years, she ended up being the #1 broker in New York, with 850 salespeople and revenue at about $97 million.

She decided to sell her business to the biggest buyer in the area, NRT, and hired an attorney to help her. When her attorney called her with the offer $20 million from NRT, she responded "Tell them I'll take $66 million" and hung up. 66 was her lucky number. Shortly after, she signed the contract for $66 million and closed two weeks later.

Chapter 10: Greedy Mindset

Most of us are guilty of wanting more. I want more. When I hit a certain level, I want to go to the next level, and then the next. That's my passion. But for some people, they get caught in this vicious cycle where wanting more becomes more important than growing, and then you hit the Greedy mindset.

In this mindset, you never achieve happiness. Despite having what you have and being where you're at, you're not satisfied with it. You're not thankful for what you have. I know this mindset very well because as I was learning and growing, I was greedy. I just wanted more and more and didn't stop to smell the roses. Later in life when I became successful and my family was making amazing residual income, we had my youngest kid. We had a great life and had plenty of money and I decided that I was going to slow down and spend time with her, more time than I spent with my older kids. See, when I was in that Greedy mindset, I sacrificed a lot of time from my older kids. I missed recitals, games, presentations, because I was out trying to become successful. There's a small advantage to the Greedy mindset, it may motivate you to become a more successful individual. But somebody had to pay a price, nothing in life is free. At that time, it was my older kid that paid the price.

It's bad when you say "I want more and I don't give a damn who I have to hurt to get it." It's ok when you say "I want more for my family." Even at a young age, that was me. I knew that for me to go up, I had to bring everyone

Chapter 10: Greedy Mindset

up with me. They say that it's lonely at the top of the mountain. Yeah if you're greedy. But if you bring the people you love with you, it's not so lonely. Home Field Advantage is key here, my family knew that I had dreams and goals and that I was going to work hard to get there. To this day, it has never been thrown at my face that I had to sacrifice being there sometimes for us to have the amazing quality of life we have.

I used the Greedy mindset to my advantage so that I could always have the drive to become successful. It wasn't that I was a greedy person, at least I don't think. I had a combination of Producer mindset and Greedy mindset, but also felt gratitude for the things that I had. Without feeling gratitude, you may fall into that trap of never being satisfied. I was able to mature in business and in life. I got involved in a business where you're not successful unless you help others become successful. That taught me so much about helping other people, helping them where they wanted to go.

But the big disadvantage is that your Greedy mindset could be the death of you. Imagine neglecting your family and friends for so long that they don't remember what it's like to be around you.

I know people who just go, go, go, and never grow. They seem to be always producing and always moving in whatever direction they're going but remember, someone somewhere in their life is paying the price. These people don't mature, they'll sacrifice everything forever. One main

Chapter 10: Greedy Mindset

trait with the Greedy mindset is that you're not focused on helping others.

I believe to get out of the Greedy mindset, you need to grow. That's what I did. I needed to expand my mind and read books, listen to audios, go to the seminars from the amazing personal development people writing those books. I realized that if I want to go up in life, I needed to mature and grow and that's what people who are in the Greedy mindset are missing. There needs to be a line drawn as to what you are willing to lose because of your greed. Once you draw that line, you're able to look at what you have and feel gratitude towards it. I've known people that have lost their whole family due to the Greedy mindset. They stayed in the Greedy mindset and never matured. Those are bad people, they'll hurt people. It's all about them. It's Me.Com.

Chapter 10: Greedy Mindset

CHAPTER REVIEW

- It's ok to want more in your life but when it becomes more important than growing, you hit the Greedy mindset.
- In this mindset, you're never happy because you're not thankful.
- Although the Greedy mindset can be motivating for you, SOMEONE is paying the price for your greed.
- In the Greedy mindset, you're not focused on helping others.
- To get out of this mindset, you need to grow.

Chapter 10: Greedy Mindset

CHAPTER 11

GRATITUDE MINDSET

Chris Gardener

The story of Chris Gardener was chronicled in one of the most inspiring movies in history, **The Pursuit of Happyness**. He wrote his autobiography to shed light on his early struggles and failures in life, which resulted in an immense amount of pain.

Gardener had a rough upbringing. With a father that wasn't present, his mother and siblings suffered abuse at the hands of his stepfather. In and out of the foster care system, Gardener was at the mercy of an unstable childhood.

Working as a research lab assistant at UCSF didn't pay enough to help support his family. In 1981, his son, Christopher Gardner Jr. was born. This led to the decision to become a medical-equipment salesman.

Gardener struggled but was committed to living life that didn't involve so much struggle. He met a man driving a red Ferrari who led him on a career path to become a stockbroker. During that journey, he suffered through an eviction and homelessness, jail and an eventual divorce. But through hard work and dedication, he achieved his dreams.

Chapter 11: Gratitude Mindset

A lot of people forget to be grateful for everything they have in life. The roof over your head, the people that live with you, your parents, your significant other, your kids, your job, your work, your health, those are all things to be grateful for. If you were born in the USA like I was, we both have access to the same basic resources. If you can be grateful for what you have, you'll never take anything for granted and be happy in life.

People in the Gratitude mindset appreciate the things they have a lot more and it keeps them humble, no matter how much success they have in life. They also make the most out of the precious time that they have. I still haven't found any disadvantages to being in the Grateful mindset.

There's a reason I put this chapter right after the Greed mindset: it's because the Gratitude mindset can snap you out of the Greed mindset. When I was young, I just wanted more and more and more. I started getting cars and houses and acquiring business. I learned over time that you need to take yourself out of your situation and look at it from the outside, look at it from afar. When I learned how to do that, I realized that I was grateful. I sometimes have to remind my wife about this. "I know we want more, a bigger house, more stuff, live in a bigger community but we have to be grateful for what we have, be grateful for our children, our beautiful house, our freedom, time, money." I'm not saying that we have all this stuff because I'm trying to impress you. I'm saying this because I'm trying to impress upon you the fact that, that wasn't me when I first

Chapter 11: Gratitude Mindset

started out, I wasn't in the Gratitude mindset. I would look at what I had and it would frustrate me because I didn't have more. The "things" I kept acquiring were cool and made me want even more "things."

It was when I got time plus freedom when I appreciated what I already had. I truly believe that anything worthwhile is uphill. You have to grind and be in the Producer and Greedy mindset a little bit when you're first starting out because your Dreamer mindset has some crazy goal that you're just waiting to hit. But it's only when you're able to have some time freedom that you're able to look back on things and switch into the Gratitude mindset and feel thankful for what you've accomplished, for what your family has accomplished.

If you're a real estate agent who wants to be a broker and have many agents working with you, be grateful that you're able to sell houses, some people don't even sell one. If you have a mid-tier job at an office and you're waiting for a promotion, be grateful that you even have a job, some people can't work and support themselves. If you're a college student that's studying for finals, be grateful that you're even at college, some people can't afford to learn. If you're in a relationship and things are a little bit rocky right now because of some argument, look at the relationship and be grateful for the good things and build from that. If you're on a basketball team on the bench but you're upset that you aren't starting, be grateful that you worked hard and got on the team. If you're a

Chapter 11: Gratitude Mindset

musician playing some dive bar in Downtown LA, be grateful that you even got a gig, a lot of musicians never do.

When I was growing up in the nasty parts of LA, I didn't know we were poor. I didn't know we didn't have money, I was kid, how could I know what that meant? When I had to climb a tree to find the perfect branches so I could make a slingshot, that was just fun, I didn't realize we couldn't afford a slingshot. We were happy kids and we had fun. We played baseball and football in the street where cars would go up and down. We had parks nearby, you just never ever wanted to go to the ones near where I grew up. Here's the point I'm trying to make, we were happy, we were grateful.

When I got older, I realized, maybe this wasn't the best place to raise a kid; I wanted more. That's the thing, I have always been able to look back on my circumstances that I grew up in and be grateful that I wasn't dead or in jail and that things were only going to get better from here. I also realized that along my journey to success, there's people that have helped me get to where I am. My parents, my family, my brothers, my mentors, even the people that were trying to bring me down. It's a great place to be when you are able to look at the world you've created around you and be grateful for what it took to get there and grateful for just being there.

I'll talk about the Jealous mindset in a few chapters but one very important thing about the Grateful mindset is that

Chapter 11: Gratitude Mindset

you are happy for others. When someone that you know has some success, you root for them and cheer for them. You don't get jealous because they have some sort of success, you are grateful that they're able to have that success. You live a much happier life being grateful.

If you have any sort of upbringing like I did, you appreciate that you're still here and working on your life. And if you didn't, be grateful that you didn't have to go through that and work hard to keep it so you don't ever have to. Some people may have to go through some drama or trauma in life to feel grateful.

When I became successful, I was able to buy my dad an RV and my mom a brand new Mercedes. I was able to take them on vacations and family trips all over the world. My mom and dad were always there for me, despite what was around us and what we could afford, they were there for me. I am so grateful to them for being there and supporting me that I want to give them the world. I was able to invest in a business with my brother. I took nieces, nephews, cousins on family vacations. Understand this, the more successful you become, the more it impacts the people around you, your Home Field. Be grateful that you're having success and that you have those closest to you along for the ride cheering you on.

Chapter 11: Gratitude Mindset

CHAPTER REVIEW

- People in the Gratitude mindset appreciate things they have and remain humble.
- You also make the most out of the time you have because you appreciate it.
- You need to take yourself out of the situation and look at it from afar to be grateful.
- Everything worthwhile is uphill.
- It's great when you can look at what you've created around you and the struggle it was to get there.
- Root for others, be grateful that someone else is shooting for their dreams too.
- Remember the people that have come along for the ride, be grateful they were and still are there for you, cheering you on.

CHAPTER 12

CONFIDENT MINDSET

The Beatles

Even though they have sold over 1.6 billion records worldwide, The Beatles once considered themselves failures. On New Year's Eve in 1961, the group drove in a snowstorm to Decca Recording Studios to lay down 15 tracks based on songs that they were already performing.

It was Dick Rowe, a talent scout, that was there to hear their sound, who stated that they would never succeed. Specifically, he said that "guitar groups were on their way out." Five months later, the group received the big break they had been hoping to receive. and signed with George Martin from Parlophone and released their first in a string of hits late that year entitled, "Love Me Do."

While others might have gotten discouraged during the rejections and the failures faced by the group, The Beatles didn't throw in the towel. They knew deep down inside that they were bound to be famous and that it was just a matter of time as long as they didn't give up.

Chapter 12: Confident Mindset

Confidence is the key to action and happiness. How confident we are has a huge effect on our mental health, our ability to be social, how we think about ourselves, and our belief in our capabilities. When you're confident, you're more likely to take action on your goals.

I've been pretty confident in my life but I do remember times where getting into the Confident mindset was a struggle. When I first started out in business, there were a ton of things that I didn't know and even more things that I didn't know that I didn't know. There were times where I had to go meet with people who were way more successful than me and I just wasn't at their level. I had confidence but I was super shaky because it was new. The thing is, I was confident in my ability to figure it out. I knew me, and I could control me. The shakiness came from the unknown. But as I grew and matured, confidence came naturally.

I had a mentor that used to say "when you walk into a room, pretend like you own the place." You know, it's funny how much you hear that statement from fake hustlers on social media. But it's really important WHO that statement is coming from. My mentor said that when you walk into a room, greet people, look them in the eye, acknowledge and listen, and respect people. Go up to them and say your name, "nice to meet you…" as if you were the owner of the place. You don't walk in to a room thinking that you're better than everyone, the Confidence mindset lets you know that you don't have to compare yourself to

Chapter 12: Confident Mindset

anyone at all. Just make a presence and people will gravitate towards you, it's the Law of Attraction.

I remember in sales how I went into every potential sale: I would say "I'm going to sell 10 of this thing" and that's the state of mind I carried throughout my conversations with people. I would psych myself up to go there and get it done. Another way I would psych myself up, and I recommend this to everyone, is to dress confidently. Look good, feel good, do good. Wearing clothing that you're comfortable in will make you feel good and give you the confidence that you need to be productive and close the deal.

People want to be around confident people that know where they're going. That's my #1 secret to success: If people don't know where you're going, they're not going to follow you. If you're confident in what you're doing, where you're going, and the goals that you have, people would be afraid NOT to follow you.

Now, a big disadvantage to the Confident mindset is when you cross that threshold into arrogance. Who would you rather work with at a job: Person A who comes in smiling, dressed nice, who always says hello to people and calls them by their name, or Person B who just comes in straight to their workspace like they're better than you. That's the line between confidence and arrogance.

The Confident mindset is key also in relationships. I've met MANY people that say that they were attracted to their significant other's confidence more than anything else.

Chapter 12: Confident Mindset

They weren't a super model or had a bunch of cash, they were just confident. They would rather be with the confident person instead of looking for the super model that lacked confidence. I remember growing up with this one friend. He was a slightly heavyset guy but he had these colored eyes. This guy's confidence was through the roof! I think he thought he looked like Brad Pitt. This guy was so confident that he would date the most beautiful women in the school. It was crazy! There were guys working out, doing sports that were fit but they weren't confident and couldn't even match what this guy was doing. He just walked around like he was 'THE GUY.'

I know many business people that have used music to get them into the state of mind they needed right before doing something a little scary. I recommend doing this: if you have a presentation or something that you're about to do, as you practice to get it right, play a certain song in the background, your favorite hype song. Play it every single time that you're practicing. When you go to do the presentation, play it right before. All the information you study and practiced will come back to you as an emotion and give you the confidence in yourself because you know that you know the presentation. It's all a psychology that you build for yourself when it doesn't come naturally. Psych yourself up to be confident.

I remember growing up, I always had confidence. Whether or not I succeeded was another thing, but I had the confidence. If I was playing basketball and we needed

Chapter 12: Confident Mindset

to shoot the last shot, I would ask for the ball so I could shoot it. Whether I missed it or not, I had the confidence that I could do it. Sometimes I'd make it and sometimes I'd miss and then I'd have to deal with the consequences… but when it came time to take the shot, I shot it and I owned it.

The key if you're having trouble being confident is taking care of yourself first. I'll give you an example. When I was first starting out in business, I had to make sales calls. I would shower, get dressed, do my hair, put on dress shoes, and wear cologne… to do sales calls where no one would ever see me. The reason I did that was because I wanted to sound confident on the phone and I knew that if I looked good and felt good that I would do good. I would even look in the mirror while I spoke, I just wanted to make sure that the person on the other side of the phone was receiving it the right way. And eventually, I didn't have to do those things anymore, the confidence came naturally. But at first, that was a major help to my confidence.

This is another key mindset where Home Field Advantage can boost it. If you're reading this book or listening to this audio, remember that if you have a spouse that is trying to make it happen, your positivity and belief in them instills confidence in them, too. Support them to build their confidence. I always tell my wife and kids, "Go out there. You got this, you can do this. Conquer it." It works wonders for their confidence knowing that they have the support of the ones they love.

Chapter 12: Confident Mindset

Now, if you have a big ego, that's where the arrogance can come into play. Confidence is interesting this way, it can really show someone's true colors once they become confident. Think about this: if you're confident in who you are, you are more likely to show to other people who you are. That's when you see the confident humble people separated from the confident arrogant people. You can see what kind of person someone is by the way that they treat the workers, the servers, the bus boy, and the staff. You can spot the arrogant people that think that they're better than the people that work there, and you can spot the people that respect others around them.

Chapter 12: Confident Mindset

CHAPTER REVIEW

- Confidence is the key to action and happiness.
- When you're confident, you're more likely to take action on your goals.
- We fear the unknown.
- When you walk into a room, pretend like you're the owner. Greet people, look them in the eye, acknowledge and listen to them, respect them.
- Psych yourself up before doing something scary. You may want to have "your song" that you play before doing certain things.
- People want to be around confident people.
- Take care of yourself. Dress up even for just a phone call.
- If you have an ego, you can become arrogant and come across as disrespectful to others. Don't do that.

Chapter 12: Confident Mindset

CHAPTER 13

JEALOUS MINDSET

Shawn Carter aka Jay-Z

Jay-Z is an American singer, songwriter and entrepreneur who's sold over 100 million records and rose up against the odds to succeed in life. While quite possibly considered one of the most famous and successful rappers of all time, his early life was dominated by failures and an unstable family life that led to him to sell drugs.

Carter grew up in housing projects. After his father had abandoned the family, it was his mother that raised him and his three siblings. He became passionate about music early on. However, while wanting to pursue a record career, he realized that no label wanted to sign him, so he opted instead to sell CDs out of the trunk of his car. Every major label had turned him down, so he did what any enterprising young individual would do that was committed to succeeding – he co-founded his own label!

Eventually, Jay-Z released his debut album entitled, Reasonable Doubt, which reached number 23 on the Billboard 200, and it eventually hit platinum, with Rolling Stone calling it one of the 500 greatest albums of all time. This was the start of a long and very successful career.

Chapter 13: Jealous Mindset

The Jealous mindset is basically when you look at other people and you're jealous because they might have more success than you. They may have more wealth, better health, a better relationship, or a better body.

The one cool thing about the Jealous mindset is that it can motivate you and push you towards action. Especially if you combine this mindset with something like Producer and Gratitude mindset.

The bad thing about being in this mindset is that you waste so much time comparing yourself to others, and today, this one is so prominent in anyone that uses social media. You can become obsessed with what they're doing on there and could even think of other people in a negative way, just because you're being jealous.

Go on social media right now, Facebook, Instagram, whatever and look at what people are posting. 99% of what people are posting will lean towards 'look at me, look at what I'm doing.' People don't post their struggles. It's like looking at informercials all day. Imagine you're sitting at your job right now and you scroll through post after post of people celebrating new things they got, new places they're going, new things they got to do, and new people they're hanging out with. Look at how much fun they're having! It's a farce! But the way it affects you, you start thinking things like man, "Why can't I be on that vacation?" or "Why can't I get that thing?" Just scrolling through social media while you're at work can build your Jealous mindset and just eat away at you.

Chapter 13: Jealous Mindset

Look, I get it. A lot of people want more. They want to "Keep up with the Joneses." You see that your neighbor got a new car, maybe we should get a new car. Or your neighbor added on to their house, maybe we should add on to our house. I've seen people make huge financial mistakes with this Jealous mindset.

When I was growing up, maybe like Junior High, my friends and I didn't want luxury brands. We didn't really see a lot of people with luxury brands so we didn't really care. But now, you can find posts from your favorite brand ambassadors sporting those cute new kicks and think to yourself "Man, I need to get those so I can be more like them." I can see social media creating people with the Jealous mindset. What you don't realize when you see those posts is how fake those posts are. It's ok to see these things and maybe get inspired or get into the Dreamer mindset of wanting something like the people you see on social media, but it's when you start obsessing over those things and get into the Jealous mindset that puts you down. All day long.

I remember I was part of a business where people my age and maybe a little younger were having more success than me. Seeing them excel where I didn't, it made me jealous. It would eat me up and it wasn't healthy. The thing is, their success had nothing to do with me. It was THEIR own timing. I didn't understand at first that success is a process where I needed to learn, fail, learn, grow, learn, and succeed. I don't know what these people went

Chapter 13: Jealous Mindset

through, or the hurdles they had to jump over to get to where they were at. But seeing them excel would still bother me. It was a while before I learned to celebrate other people's success instead of being jealous of their success.

Now, if someone comes in to my business and does better than me, I celebrate it. I'm happy for them. That's because it shows the potential for our business and what can be achieved in a relatively short amount of time. They can do it faster than I did! And that's what's happening in the business world nowadays, people are joining business now with the technology that is available and hitting milestones way faster than any of us did without that technology. The ME now, celebrates and applauds at what can be done because that means other people can do it, too. The ME back then might have let their success completely eat them up.

I was never a "show me" type of person, a boastful person. In the business I'm in, people want to see the success of others so they can see what is possible for them. I tell my story, post my success and the success of people on my team on social media, not to be boastful but to be hopeful. The thing is, I see how some people can get into the Jealous mindset from something like that. If you're in a position where you can influence people like that, be responsible and realize that you can be having this kind of effect on people.

Chapter 13: Jealous Mindset

How do you get out of being in the Jealous mindset? Ask people how they did it. "What did you do?" If you're jealous of someone that reaches a certain position at your job, ask them how they got there. If you're in the minor leagues and want to play in the majors, send a message to a Major League player from their website or on Twitter and ask them how they did it. When you turn the Jealous mindset into a place of growth and learning, you can learn to be genuinely happy for people and turn your Jealous mindset into something more productive. A lot of people's ego won't even allow them to humble themselves like that. Those are the kind of people that need to get into the Development mindset (we'll talk about that in a later chapter.)

CHAPTER REVIEW

- The Jealous mindset can motivate you and push you towards action.
- But it can be bad if you spend your time comparing yourself to others.
- Don't become obsessed on social media. People only post the positive things they do. They don't post all the negative stuff.
- Other people's successes have nothing to do with you. If you're jealous about someone's success, ask them how they did it. That's the best way to turn that feeling into something positive.
- Celebrate others, don't be jealous about it.
- Humble and grow yourself out of this mindset.

CHAPTER 14

LAZY MINDSET

Sophia Amoruso

Diagnosed with ADHD at an early age and withdrawn from school as a result, Amoruso spent her formative years working odd jobs; following her parents' divorce, she then relocated to Sacramento, CA, where she claims to have survived by hitchhiking, shoplifting and stealing from bins.

The San Diego native managed to catch a break in 2006, however, when she started selling vintage clothing and other items through her eBay account under the guise of Nasty Gal Vintage (so named after a Betty Davis record); its revenue subsequently grew from $223,000 in 2008 to nearly $23m in 2011, leading to her being dubbed the "Cinderella of tech" by the New York Times.

Amoruso has also written a book about her experiences (which was later commissioned by Netflix into a full-length TV series), and although she has since stepped down as CEO of Nasty Gal, the company made $20m from its sale to retail giants Boohoo. In 2017, Amoruso founded Girlboss Media, a lifestyle website for millennial women.

Chapter 14: Lazy Mindset

Being lazy is one of the worst mindsets that is actually super popular today. It has no discipline, no desire to get off your ass and do something. Yeah, if you're idle or lazy, it's easy to achieve happiness in the short-term. But you're less likely to possess the discipline to achieve big things. Look, there's totally a place and time to BE lazy. To watch your favorite TV show or to just slouch around. But some people make that into an entire mindset where they do that all the time. Do you know someone that comes home and watches TV until they go to sleep? That's who I'm talking about.

I remember that when I first started out in business, I didn't want to fall into that trap so what we did is we cut out the cable TV in the house so that there was no TV. We cut out the thing that would make us lazy. The Kardashians aren't going to pay for my kid's college tuition, that's for sure. So I need to cut it out and be productive. I read books and listened to audiobooks instead because you should always be growing and learning. There's so much personal development out there for you. What happens next on The Voice isn't going to benefit you unless you're actually on the show.

I like to prioritize my time. I make sure that business is done, family is good, and that I've taken care of myself before I do something like veg out in front of the TV. I actually make it a habit to only watch my favorite shows when I'm traveling up in the plane since I have no where to go, can't make any phone calls, and can't do much else. If

Chapter 14: Lazy Mindset

you don't travel, maybe prioritize your day, take care of things and then watch it late at night when everyone is asleep. But some people let these habits consume them daily. I KNOW people that while at work, watch a full TV show. Again, if your work allows for you to listen to an audiobook while you're working, more power to you. But watching or listening to stuff like that takes your full attention when you should be working or getting things done. This is the same with social media. The new age TV is just scrolling on social media.

If you have a Lazy mindset, you're not going to be successful. But here's the thing, I've seen it and experienced it where making a lot of passive income can put you in the Lazy mindset, too. I could see someone in the Producer mindset fall right into the Lazy mindset after some time. People get tired and burnt out. We all do. And it's fine to get a little lazy, that's what a lazy weekend is. But come Monday, you gotta switch it back on and get things done. If you have a lot of time freedom, you gotta find something productive to fill those gaps for you.

I can almost guarantee you that there are athletes out there that could have been the next elite all star... but they got lazy. I'm not going to name any specific people but there have been rookie players that get their dream signings onto teams, have a good couple of months and then never do anything again. That kind of mindset puts you into a false sense of accomplishment and then you become satisfied with the short-term. What happens next

Chapter 14: Lazy Mindset

season? What about 5 years from now? Those players could have become all-stars but they got into the Lazy mindset. They're such good players that they get by just on their talent and aren't willing to put in the work after hours to be elite. The people who aren't willing to do that extra phone call or do that extra meeting or go that extra mile on their marriage anniversary, they could have been great if they weren't lazy.

Then time when I cut off the TV at my house, that was super hard for me because I love sports. I couldn't watch the games! And back then, I couldn't just load up an app on my phone and find out the score. What I did was after the day was done, I'd go to a restaurant or bar that had the game playing and catch the end of the game then go home. I didn't have it consuming me all day long.

Maybe if you're addicted to your phone or social media, maybe go out and get an old-school flip phone. If it's TV for you, maybe take some sheets of paper and write some goals on them and cover your TV. As you complete the goals, you get parts of the screen back.

And here's the thing, you need your outlets in life. The classic "All work and no play makes Jack a dull boy." I'm not saying don't have those things. I'm just saying that if you want be successful, be productive during the Prime Time and have your outlets in the Down Time.

CHAPTER REVIEW

- The Lazy mindset has no discipline and no desire to do something.
- There may be things in your life that you're putting so much time into that you're not doing other things. You may need to cut some stuff out.
- Prioritize your time to get out of this mindset.
- If you have a Lazy mindset, you're not going to be successful.
- Everyone needs to have their outlets in life. Just be productive during Prime Time and have your outlets in the Down Time.

Chapter 14: Lazy Mindset

CHAPTER 15

BUSINESS MINDSET

Jan Koum

Born in the then-Soviet Union, Koum moved with his mother and grandmother to California in 1992, where a social support program initiated by the state allowed the family to receive a small apartment. At the age of 16, the young entrepreneur took a cleaning job at a grocery store to help support his mother. After teaching himself how to code, he then spent 9 years at Yahoo as an infrastructure engineer.

However, Koum's eureka moment came in 2009 when he realized the potential of Apple's then-fledgeling app store. The mastermind created WhatsApp a week later, utilizing the ability to push notification apps on iPhones and establishing the app as an alternative to traditional SMS messaging. In 2014, Mark Zuckerberg became interested, with Facebook acquiring WhatsApp for $19 Billion and appointing Koum to its board of directors.

Although Koum stepped down from his role in April 2018 (forfeiting an estimated $1 Billion of stock in the process), he is estimated to have personally amassed over $9 Billion from his work.

Chapter 15: Business Mindset

Many of you reading this book are wanting to get into business, to be entrepreneurs. Or maybe you already own your own business. The Business mindset is not just for entrepreneurs. You love to provide a service to people and help change the world. With this mindset, you can help others and you can solve difficult problems.

I got into business because I wanted financial independence and time freedom. I was tired of people telling me what time I should wake up in the morning to go to work. I got tired of people telling me what time I was going to get hungry. I didn't like people telling me what time I was going to stop being hungry. I remember on several occasions that I had to sit at a drive thru for about 95% of my lunch, and then had to basically drink my food because I only had a few minutes left.

I didn't necessarily know it, but my first business was in the business of helping other people. While achieving my dreams, I was helping other people do the same thing. Now that I've been able to make enough money to have independence, I wanted to teach others to do the same. I turned my passion into profits then turned all of it into teaching others.

Some people can focus too much on making money and not focus on the passion. That's the negative side of this mindset. There's a lot of responsibility that comes with owning a business and if you don't take care of your business and just worry about making money, there's no long term success to be had.

Chapter 15: Business Mindset

The Business mindset is a leadership mindset and uses many of the other mindsets in this book. If you have a business and someone doesn't show up for work, they call in sick, what are you gonna do? Or a delivery of some important material didn't come in, what are you going to do? You have no choice but to take care of it, even if you have employees, you have more to lose than any of them because the business is yours. You have to be ready to wear all the hats in the business until you're ready to hire people to handle stuff for you. You may not be good and you may not want to do those things but that's what being a business owner is all about, having the responsibility and the leadership to serve others via your business.

Imagine if after starting your own business to create financial independence for you and your family, you're able to support charities that you're passionate about, help out family members, sponsor local youth teams, help out your community, and mentor others? This is the what it means to turn your passion into profits. Your mindset of wanting to provide a service to people and help change the world can open up doors to all the things you couldn't do before.

CHAPTER REVIEW

- The Business mindset loves serving others.
- This is a leadership mindset where you can help others and solve difficult problems.
- The Business mindset wears many hats, especially if you're running your own business.

CHAPTER 16

FEAR MINDSET

Jack Ma

When it comes to taking a hint, few can match the stubbornness of Jack Ma; after graduating in 1988 (a process that he was initially rejected four times for), the Hangzhou native struggled to find work, getting turned down by over 30 companies (including, infamously, KFC), before seeing all 10 of his postgraduate applications to Harvard Business School refused.

However, on a 1995 trip to visit friends in the US, Ma's luck finally changed; after being introduced to the internet, he managed to raise $20,000 to build an online directory for Chinese businesses, taking on various web projects for Chinese companies and government organizations. Utilizing these experiences, he returned to China in 1999 and created the online marketplace Alibaba, subsequently raising $25 billion at its IPO stock exchange offering in 2014.

Ma is now one of the richest people in the world, with an estimated personal net worth of nearly $43 billion, while the Alibaba group is responsible for nine major subsidiaries (among them the hugely popular Aliexpress).

Chapter 16: Fear Mindset

We all have a little fear inside of us. But when you let the fears consume you and become your everyday, that's when you're in the Fear mindset. People who let fear get the best of them aren't able to use their time to the best of their ability. I don't see any advantages to this mindset. But the disadvantages are immense, you can never achieve your dreams by being in fear.

Fear stands for False Evidence Appearing Real. Fear is interesting because we all have it in different capacities. Someone may have a fear of failing in their goals. Someone else might have a fear of striking out with someone they have a crush on. But I think we all have a slight fear of the unknown. Even successful people have that. It just depends on how you react to it. If you let the fear paralyze you, you let it win.

I have learned that the more you do what you fear, the less you fear it. Let's take the fear of public speaking as an example. I have helped so many people become successful public speakers. That success comes from starting small, doing small speaking engagements in living rooms, small gatherings, and stuff like that. Then we move on to events at hotels, then it moves to stadiums.

When I first started to speak publicly, I had fear. I had a business partner years ago who was going to help do a presentation for me… but they didn't show up. I had to do it and I was nervous as hell. I even wrote bullet points on my hand that ended up getting smeared off with how much I was sweating due to the fear. But I did the

Chapter 16: Fear Mindset

presentation. I don't remember what I said or how I did, but I remember after doing it thinking "I can do this, that wasn't so bad." Once you do it and get over it, it's not as bad as you thought it would be.

When I was in little league baseball, I remember a lot of kids were afraid to get hit by the ball. They would go up to bat and be afraid of getting hit so they struck out. That same principle applies to us adults. A lot of people go through life worrying about what can go wrong instead of worrying about what can go right. Yeah, you could get hit by the ball… but what if you hit a home run? That fear can dictate your outcome.

Even people who are somewhat successful can live in the Fear mindset. The one thing that is keeping them safe is their fear. There's the bottom which is complete fear and no success, there's the middle which is the safe zone, and there's the top which is massive success. For many people, the fear of hitting the bottom doesn't allow them to hit the top. I have relatives that had fear of investing in things and fear of owning their own business.

Just by you reading this book, I know that you want to be successful. I'm not saying that people who play it safe have a bad life. Playing it safe is, well, safe. You can have Gratitude and be Productive in the safe zone with whatever fears you have. But for you, reading this book wanting to be successful in whatever it is that you're trying to achieve, you have to face that fear. If you fear flying, go on a short flight and move up from there. If you fear rejection for a

Chapter 16: Fear Mindset

relationship, go ask people that you may be interested in you to go have some coffee or tea. Because one will conquer the other: either the fear will be conquered by you facing it or the fear will conquer you. If you want to be successful, face it and conquer it.

Chapter 16: Fear Mindset

CHAPTER REVIEW

- People in the Fear mindset let fear control their lives.
- The more you do what you fear, the less you'll fear it.
- Don't worry about what can go wrong. Instead, think about what can go right.
- For many people, the fear of hitting rock bottom doesn't allow them to hit the top.
- If you want to be successful, you need to face your fears because either the fear will conquer you or you will conquer the fear.
- You can never achieve your dreams by being in fear.

Chapter 16: Fear Mindset

CHAPTER 17

NETWORKING MINDSET

Sarah Jessica Parker

Parker was born in a poor coal-mining town in rural Ohio, the youngest of four children. Her parents divorced when she was two, and her mother remarried shortly thereafter and had an additional four children. Parker's stepfather, a truck driver, was often out of work, so the future starlet took up singing and dancing at a very young age to help supplement her mom's teaching income and feed their 10-person family.

Despite hard times and occasionally being on welfare, Parker's mom continued to encourage her children's interest in the arts. The family moved to Cincinnati, where Parker was enrolled in a ballet, music, and theater school on scholarship. When she was 11 years old, the family took a trip to New York City so Parker could audition for a Broadway play. The trip was a success—she and her brother were both cast, and the family relocated to New York. Parker continued to work hard and land roles, eventually becoming the title character of TV juggernaut Sex and the City.

Chapter 17: Networking Mindset

My dad is probably the most social person that I know. He can go anywhere at anytime and make friends with everybody. People love him and he has friends everywhere! And that's where my social skills came from, they got passed to me by my dad. I know this because my mom is the complete opposite. She doesn't speak to strangers and just doesn't want to so I grew up with the two sides of being social.

People who have the Networking mindset love to hang around with people, make new friends, and discover new cultures. They say your netWORK determines the size of your net WORTH and if you don't have a good network, you have to switch into the Networking mindset and put yourself into a good network. But if you rely on talking to others for happiness, you won't get anywhere.

The person in the Networking mindset can be put anywhere. That's the kind of person you want to put in the front of the room for a presentation. And for me, even though I may have gotten the gift of gab from my father, I still wasn't the guy that was going to go out there and talk to complete strangers. That actually made it hard when I got into direct sales because that's the kind of business where you HAVE to talk to complete strangers to build your network. But I knew that if I wanted to grow my business the way that I wanted to, I had to get out of my shell and go talk to people.

Especially paired with the Business mindset, you have to be a networker if you want your business to grow. Think

Chapter 17: Networking Mindset

about it, if you're a businessperson, you want your doors open to bring new business for yourself. Let's say that you have an Italian restaurant nearby. At some point when you're out and about, you may have an opportunity to talk to complete strangers. If you insert it into the conversation that you own an Italian restaurant, tell them that if they come by, you'll give them a discount. Then those people come to your restaurant, love the food, and then tell their friends. You just opened up an unlimited amount of potential customers to your restaurant just by speaking to complete strangers. What if you're a contractor and you're at your kid's soccer game and there are other parents around you. Introduce yourself, share what you do. What if those people were looking to add a patio to their house and you didn't even know? Then they refer you because they like you and do good work.

And I don't think I have to even say it but what about relationships? If you get yourself into a Networking mindset, you will talk to more people and open up the doors to someone that may be the perfect person for you.

The Networking mindset pretty much can cover any aspect of life that you want to be successful at, you just gotta insert yourself into situations where you can grow your network.

Chapter 17: Networking Mindset

CHAPTER REVIEW

- Your NetWORK determines your net WORTH.
- People in the Networking mindset love to be around people.
- But sometimes, they can rely on others for happiness.
- This type of mindset is best if you have to be in front of the room for a presentation.
- If you're a business owner, this mindset is key to growing your business.
- This mindset can work in all aspects of life.

CHAPTER 18

DEVELOPMENT MINDSET

Richard Branson

Richard Branson has seemingly (and successfully) tried his hand at every possible line of investment across the last 40 years - not bad for a man who performed poorly at school and was diagnosed with dyslexia.

The importing and re-selling of music records was his first venture. Alongside the management of the popular Student magazine, he was hugely successful. As a result, Branson was able to open a dedicated record store in London in 1971. He used the profits from this project to establish Virgin Records, working with many of the artists that he'd previously interviewed for Student, such as the Rolling Stones.

From there, Branson has created and developed market leading products and services in aviation, media, beverages and rail transport among many others; his personal net worth is estimated to be around $4.9 Billion, as he constantly seeks to invest his profits from one venture into another.

Chapter 18: Development Mindset

People in the Development mindset are growing. They challenge themselves to be better than they were yesterday. People who have the desire to grow are always developing themselves. They look at a situation and think that it could always be better somehow. It's going to be a lot easier for them to put in the work needed to succeed. They just can't be so set on growing that they forget living.

Before becoming an entrepreneur, I wasn't growing myself. I did zero personal development. The only thing I had was the circumstances I grew up in, and I used those things to mold me into the person I was at the time. I got good out of that for sure. But I never knew that there was more that I could become. When I started reading books, I started learning concepts I never knew about… and I hated reading, but I loved growing. I only really ever read the sports pages before that, but I remember the first books I read, I thought to myself "Wait a minute, they're talking about me," and that made it more interesting to me and I got excited to read.

And here's the interesting part: as I started to learn more, my circle of influence started changing. I started hanging out with those people that would challenge me to become more than I already was. I was even attracting different kinds of people to my business. It's called the Law of Attraction, you become that kind of person you want to attract to your network. I became more focused and more consistent as I grew which led more people to be attracted to me and what I was doing.

Chapter 18: Development Mindset

My personal mentor at the time was John C Maxwell. He didn't know he was my mentor, I had never met him. All I did was read his books. I remember reading a book called Failing Forward that taught me that even though I failed at different aspects of my life, it was ok. I thought that I would be a baseball player and then I didn't. I thought I was going to go to school but instead I got kicked out. I thought many things that didn't come to be and I felt like I let my family, my parents down. Failing Forward helped me grow past that. It talked about using failure as fertilizer and understand that as long as you learn and grow from the failure, you can go out and be successful. I'm 5'9" tall. I learned that if I fall flat on my face, I'm 5'9" closer to my dreams and goals, I just gotta get up and do it.

These kinds of books helped me grow and gave me the belief that even I could go and hit that next level in life and become successful. If you want to be the greatest version of yourself, you need to get into the Development mindset and grow.

There are two problems with being in the Development mindset though. One, you are growing so much that you forget to live your life. Don't miss the moments in life that become beautiful memories because you were so set on following some sort of exercise from a book. And Two, I've seen many people grow so much and continue growing… but never do anything. They read the books, listen to the

Chapter 18: Development Mindset

audios, do the exercises, but never apply the things they learned. Grow, learn, then apply it.

It's kind of like when I was in construction. I had to go to a trade school to learn some of the things I needed to know for construction work, reading blue prints and whatnot. I learned more at the actual job than I did at the school. I had to go to school as the requirement to learn whatever facts but I only learned how to actually do it at the job. It's the same thing with the Development mindset. You grow but then you learn and apply it to your life.

When I read Failing Forward, it made me want to read the next one, and then the next one. It changed my way of thinking. I remember when my oldest kid got accepted to Stanford University. He was in high school and I knew he needed to prepare for the world not just by what he learned in school but also by growing himself as a person. I gave him personal development books and gave him money as he read them to incentivize him to finish them. I told him "Look, the school isn't what is going to make you become successful, it's the student that becomes successful. You'll meet great people and learn great things but that doesn't matter, it's what you do with it that counts." Some people think that just by going to a great school that you're going to be a success. Not true. I didn't even graduate high school and I still became successful in business because of the Development mindset.

If you want some books to read after reading this, I'll tell you my favorites when I was growing. Think and Grow Rich

Chapter 18: Development Mindset

by Napoleon Hill, How to Win Friends and Influence People by Dale Carnegie, Failing Forward by John C Maxwell, and Rich Dad Poor Dad by Robert Kiyosaki. Those four books were four year universities for me.

Chapter 18: Development Mindset

CHAPTER REVIEW

- People in the development mindset are growing.
- This mindset allows you to look at a situation and think that it could always be better.
- Start reading more, you may be surprised learning about the things that you don't know you don't know.
- As you start to grow, your circle of influence starts changing because you want to surround yourself with people who can motivate you to achieve more.
- But as you grow, don't forget to live. Don't miss the moments in life that become beautiful memories because you were so set on following an exercise from a certain book.
- As you grow, learn, and then apply.

CHAPTER 19

BULLETPROOF MINDSET

Angel Olvera

Angel grew up in the harsh streets of Los Angeles, CA. He didn't come from money but always wanted to live a dream lifestyle. He also didn't graduate from high school but soon figured out that he had to find... something.

Angel started a career in construction and custom woodworking, exchanging his time for money to pay his family's growing bills. During that stage in his life, a co-worker introduced him to a Network Marketing business... and it changed his life. This was the vehicle that Angel was looking for so that he could work full time in his job... but part time on his dreams. A lot of time and dedication went into that business and at the age of 23, Angel hit the second highest position. He accomplished this in 6 months and has been full-time ever since.

In the last 12 years, he has helped thousands of people walk away from their jobs and experience that same lifestyle. Now, Angel Olvera owns several different types of businesses, generates millions of dollars annually throughout his networks and helps mentor people with drive and commitment to spring board their dreams and ideas into tangible success.

Chapter 19: Bulletproof Mindset

Bulletproof speaks for itself. We live in a world of negativity, cynics, people trying to bring you down, people trying to project their insecurities onto everybody else; "you can't do this, you can't do that." And then we live in a world with people on the internet showing these unrealistic lives and people trying to keep up with them. You have to have a #BulletproofMindset.

You have to know what you want, how you're gonna do it, and you need to go after it. You can't let anybody stop you from doing it. All these mindsets I've talked about in this book, the key is KNOWING which mindset you're at in this current moment, where you've been, how do you overcome, and how do you get out of it. Bulletproof is being aware. Now that you've read this book, you're aware of where you are, who you are. Maybe you didn't realize that you're in the Greedy mindset or the Lazy mindset, whatever it is. You may have not understood this before. I know because I've been there. That's why I wanted to write this book and share with people exactly where they are and how to be in the right frame of mind to do what you need to do. When I'm out doing business, I switch to the Business mindset. When I need to produce, I turn on the Producer mindset to be effective. When I'm with my family and we're in Hawaii on the beach on vacation, you better believe I'm in the Gratitude mindset.

You gotta know what mindset you need to be in for the situation you're in. That's what being bulletproof is all

Chapter 19: Bulletproof Mindset

about. Don't let anybody dictate what your mindset should be, because you are your own person.

Most people don't know what mindset they're in. Let's say somebody is out there and they're very successful and make lots of money, but they're not happy because they're in the Greed mindset and just want more money. They need to know about the Gratitude mindset to be happy.

I've had people in one of my businesses call me. That person is not a good problem solver, they're not in the Creative mindset. They call me down and out and I just remind them that they have to be bulletproof. They're letting others affect their mindset. I tell them that right now, you need a Business mindset, don't take it personally.

I suggest you find a mentor. And you don't need to physically be with that person or even talk to them, but gather all their content and learn from them. I've had mentors I've never met. I've had people come up to me wanting me to sign my other books telling me that I'm their mentor and I've never met them.

I've seen people live a stagnant life because of bad mindset. I've seen people just not succeed because of bad mindset. Remember the little kid that could have been the next grammy wining artist but they got told that they're being too loud? That kid is probably all grown up now, hating their job, ok with their stagnant life when they could have been something else, or that kid that was bouncing the ball could have been the next Tom Brady but someone put that doubt in their mind and that was it.

Chapter 19: Bulletproof Mindset

I've learned something amazing through my ups and downs: if you put it out there into the world and work hard, it's gonna happen. Everything that I said I would do, I did. Because I was bulletproof and went after it, I did it. That was the only reason that I was successful. But don't have a Short-Term mindset. Now that you're aware of the different mindsets, know that it's a process, it takes time. Success takes time. But now, from this point forward, you can be bulletproof.

Now, you have the tools to change your mindset to be successful.

CHAPTER REVIEW

- Bulletproof mindset is being aware.
- Most people don't know what mindset they're in.
- Knowing what mindset you're in is the first step. Being able to switch between the mindsets depending on what the situation calls for is being Bulletproof.
- Find a mentor.
- If you put it out there and work hard, it's gonna happen.
- Success takes time.

#*BULLETPROOF*MINDSET

I'm going to end this book with a challenge for you. I want you to go onto social media, whichever one it is, Facebook, Twitter, Instagram. I want you take a selfie and put in the description or record a video with you saying:

"Today is the first day of my success. Today is the day I become Bulletproof." and use the hashtag **#BulletproofMindset**.

My team is going to be researching all those posts and I may end up reaching out to some of you. But more importantly, you're putting it out there. You're putting out there that you're done with not being able to grow, to reach your goals, to hit that next level that you want you and your family to be at. I can guarantee you that you'll look back on that post in the future and think to yourself, "That was the day it started."

Go out there and be bulletproof.

YOUR NOTES

YOUR NOTES

YOUR NOTES

YOUR NOTES

ANGEL OLVERA

Visit my website at www.angelolvera.com and follow me on my social media to see what I'm up to.

You can also reach my team at business@angelolvera.com or fill out the form on my website if you'd like me to speak at one of your events, from a big 10,000 seat arena to your small group of 30 people. I can help you and your team/coworkers/family/friends get started on their new careers, new professional journeys, entrepreneurial conquests, just like I did.

Thank you for reading and remember to keep that #BulletproofMindset!

www.ingramcontent.com/pod-product-compliance
Lightning Source LLC
LaVergne TN
LVHW051504070426
835507LV00022B/2909